YOU CAN'T KEEP
A GOOD GOOSE DOWN
(WOOD PIGEON)

On a crisp September morning,
Percy peered out of his nest.
He felt the season calling.
Yes, he felt it in his breast.

He knew that he was different.
He had known it from a squab.
He was not a normal pigeon.
He could feel his heartbeat throb.

His brothers and his sisters
Had long fluttered from the fold.
He missed their fluffy presence.
But he held to dreams foretold.

From slumbers he remembered
Mighty wings and deltered skeins.
And he'd known he was a gosling.
Goose blood rampaged through his veins.

He had tried to tell his family.
They agreed that he was bonkers.
But fate had come approaching
And he heard the distant honkers.

The sky was blue and cloudless
And the print of moon prevailed,
When into Percy's vision
One lone goose, majestic, sailed.

No time to pack possessions.
They would only think him soft.
He took a massive breath
And then he heaved himself aloft.

He went up like a rocket,
And was suddenly surrounded
By a broad phalanx of bodies,
And poor Perce was nearly grounded.

They shot directly past him,
In formation, like a kite.
And he madly flapped his wings
Until they disappeared from sight.

But from noises right behind him
He knew there were more to come.
Then the leader of the chevron shape
Collided with his bum.

There was a short kerfuffle,
It was quite a messy thing.
Then they realised what was happening
And took him under wing.

They said, 'We are Canadians,
But now we're national Brits.
But while the summer suits us,
Winter cold is just the pits.'

'Last year we lost poor Lucy.
And that was the final proof.
Now we're seasonally migrating.
We are off to Magaluf.'

Percy's wings were getting knackered.
He could not keep up the beat.
So they tucked him in a thermal,
Like a BA business seat.

After many hours of flying
Squadron Leader pulled the brake
And in drifts through clouds they landed
On a Balearic lake.

'You can keep your cold old Britain'
Percy cooed contentedly
As he sipped his marguerita,
As the sun sank in the sea.

GLIDERS IN THE SKY
(BUZZARD)

First day of Autumn. From our cottage door,
We tread the well-worn path into the woods.
Around us, Nature struggles to exhale
Those last, brief packages that portend life.
Not for this season do they do this thing;
But wait, in grass-stooked undergrowth, for Spring.

Out through the gate, onto the concrete road,
Left by the military, but now reclaimed,
We plunge beneath great vaults of oak and larch,
And overhead, the sky shows, patchy blue.
And there, against the dark clouds passing by,
We see the distant gliders in the sky.

Oblivious to us, they circle on.
In twos and threes, riding the thermal waves,
Too high for anything, but for the joy
Of being able to ascend so high.
We watch them, as the sun is hid by cloud,
Until they disappear through leafy shroud.

So we return. Against the dusty verge,
The bracken forests will outgrow their green
From underneath. And we'll remember well
The Autumn walks along the forest road.
And we'll recall the plaintive mewling cry
Of buzzards, regally gliding through the sky.

© September 2010

THE PELICAN AND THE ALBATROSS

Two memorable birds. They found themselves one day
Upon an island in the icy waters
Of San Francisco Bay.
The albatross perched, stately, out of reach.
The pelican performed a comic waddle
Down on the beach.

One might say 'beach', but more a strip of rock;
Forbidding place, and for the birds,
Somewhere to take stock.
The pelican looked up onto the cliff
At the gigantic bird, wind lifting pinions
In a blustery riff.

The albatross, oblivious to his neighbour, sighed
For his lost life companion and his love,
Taken by the tide.
For nothing stays the same, for beast or bird.
God only knows all tiny things
Which have occurred.

The albatross took flight. His massive wings
Casting a shadow out across the strand,
Touching the pelican. A moment's cold
Descended in a band
Of absent light. The beach bird felt the loss,
As he gazed on high, at the retreating form
Of the albatross.

The pelican resolved, although he only
Walked along this tiny island's rim,
To not be lonely.
His kind made Alcatraz their home,
Where lesser beings, unlike them,
Weren't free to roam.

© June 2021

The island of Alcatraz is named after the pelicans which have colonized
it. 'Alcatraz' is Spanish for 'pelican'. The name of the albatross comes
from similar origins, but reflects the Latin 'albus' for its white plumage.

THE BLACK-HEADED GULL

I'm a black-headed gull.
Would you ever have guessed?
If you knew who I was,
I'd be very impressed.
For all through the summer,
I'm easy to spot.
But, come the short days,
I'm decidedly not.

They call me the black-headed gull
 For a reason.
But my head plumage changes
From season to season.
Right now, like the ptarmigan,
Stoat and snow hare,
I'm trying to hide.
But it's hard, to be fair.

The problem has something
To do with my speech.
For, when I am feeding,
I let out a screech.
I never was subtle,
Or shrinking or dull.
I have shot my disguise.
I'm a black-headed gull.

© November 2020

HAVE YOU SEEN THE AVOCETS?

Have you seen the Avocets,
Those striking promenaders?
They are a bird you must not miss;
The classiest of waders.

Have you seen their pointy bills,
As fine as any chopstick
That navigates a bird's nest soup?
An avian fibre optic.

Have you seen their lovely eyes,
As polished as a berry?
Brown for girls and red for guys.
Most extraordinary!

Have you seen their slender legs
Reflected in the water?
Sometimes one, and sometimes two.
You know you really oughta.

Have you seen their little chicks
Snuggling under feather.
Tickling back of Daddy's neck,
Glad to be together?

Have you seen the avocets
When it's breeding season,
Nesting in the saline pans
For the oldest reason?

Some birds are dumpy, brown and drab,
And some are just plain brassy.
But you must see the avocet,
To view a bird that's classy.

TO A LAVEROCK
(SKYLARK)

Pity man, the earthbound,
Tied to cares and woe,
Dragged the weary world round,
Bound to bend and bow,
Unless to circle ceaselessly,
Nowhere to go.
He holds all the Earth's weight
On his slender frame,
Staggers to the last gate
Whispering his name,
Bound to corporate silence in a no-win game.
Oh to be a skylark,
Circling its way,
Cutting through the half-dark
With its lyric sway,
Pressing on the dullest sense, a potent lay.
We are small and artless,
Laverock and I.
We would not be heartless.
We were born to fly,
And with one soar illuminate the darkest sky.

© February 2000

THE CRAFT LESSON
(CUCKOO)

Carenza Cuckoo is a bird
Who's seldom seen, but often heard.
She doesn't have maternal roots;
Just drops her egg and off she scoots.
That is, until, one fateful day,
When things did not work out her way.

You see, the other birds had twigged,
And a false nesting place was rigged
Between two branches. At the base,
There was no bottom, just a space.
But, underneath, was neatly set,
A strong and many-handled net.

One morning, in the early Spring,
Carenza flew to do her thing.
She saw the nest from up on high,
And dropped, determined, from the sky.
A crafty squeeze, and out it popped.
But, through the bottom her egg dropped!

Oh dear! This was NOT what she planned.
The other birds, who were on hand,
Came hopping, when they saw her tears,
And quickly moved to calm her fears.
The egg was brought out in the net,
And, on the ground was gently set.

The birds then gathered all around
The egg, that nestled on the ground.
Carenza whimpered, 'What's the fuss'
They cried, 'Stop dumping eggs on us!'
'I cannot help it,' she confessed.
'I don't know how to build a nest.'

Then, suddenly, before she knew it,
They held a class in how to do it.
And then they built a lovely nest.
Carenza really was impressed.
'I'll build my own in yonder tree,'
'And a good mother I will be.'

THE ORDER OF THE BOOTS
(BLACKBIRD)

Blackbirds wear boots.
I think this should be known.
They're issued with them
When they're fully grown.
It is a rite of passage
From the nest.
A fledging out parade.
They've passed the test.

Our blackbird keeps his boots
So shiny clean
That they are very seldom
To be seen.
In fact, I never saw
A single pair.
It almost seems as though
They were not there.

But, come the summer,
Just past Wimbledon,
He sneaks behind a bush
And puts them on.
When strawberries ripen,
He strikes, with a whizz.
No boots on blackbirds?
Well, he sure fills his!

ALHAMBRA SKIES
(SWIFTS)

What do we expect?
The air is shimmering with heat.
The sun deigns scarily to beat
Upon the Moorish reddened
plaster walls.
Alhambra falls
Between two mountains,
Placed strategically
Because the Emir, centuries ago,
Feared not the foe,
But his own people terrified
his mind.
Two walls he built,
With soldiers in between,
And still slept fitfully inside.
And yet he couldn't hide.
It was required that he be
Conspicuously seen.
Four wives; a thousand
concubines
Floated through gardens
Perfumed with soft flowers,
And in the courtyards
Wiled away the hours
In laughter,
For their lot was silken-lined.
And, to their honeyed fate,
They were so simply,
And so beautifully resigned.
Seven hundred years.
The Emirs came and went.
And then, in 1492,
The Spanish monarchs
Took Alhambra back.
And as the Emir left,
He shed a tear,
And was, indeed, bereft.
But his hard mother
Scoffed at his regret,

And poured harsh epithets
Into his ears.
Thus, ever after,
Down those many hundred years
Her words of scorn
Have always from
Alhambra's walls
Been cruelly torn.
And now Alhambra welcomes
tourist hordes.
They climb the steps,
Invade each secret walk.
But, to my mind,
Shades of Alhambra talk,
And swifts fly deftly,
Shuttling through each
patterned arch,
As though they carried with them
Silken looms,
As in and out,
They navigate the rooms.
I trace them up
Into the azure sky
Through which these birds
So singularly fly.
I see Alhambra
Though their piercing eyes,
And feel their cries
Reverberating down
the centuries,
Until there is no time
Between the Emir's
concubines and me.
And 'Que será será,'
The whispers echo.
'What will be, will be'.

© June 2019

A KESTREL'S PRAYER

Walking to Thorley on a brisk March morning,
I saw a kestrel in a hawthorn tree.
He must have known that I was heading churchward.
I heard him whisper, 'Say a prayer for me,
For all the innocents that I have slaughtered,
And all the songs that now remain unsung,
And all the destinies that I have altered,
All be they sacrificed to feed my young.'

He floated in his majesty above me;
A fine creation of a loving Lord.
Though cruelty seemed upward in his nature,
His breathless beauty could not be ignored.
We touched upon that cold, but sunny morning,
As though his wing had brushed against my hand.
I thought, that, had he known of right and wrongness,
God would forgive, and God would understand.

© March 2006

A DIFFERENCE OF OPINION
(RAVEN & CROW)

Once there were a pair of black birds;
Ronald Raven and Vel Crow.
Both of them thought they were clever:
Nothing that they didn't know.

Ronald stated, 'I'm the bigger.'
'Therefore I've a larger brain.'
Vel retorted, 'You don't use it.'
'That, to me, is very plain.'

Ronald scoffed, 'I am historic.'
'In the Bible I am found.'
Vel sneered, 'Ever heard of Aesop?'
'I think you're on dodgy ground.'

Ronald sank to petty insults.
'You are too stuck up for words.'
'And your habits are atrocious.'
'You give a bad name to birds.'

Vel said, 'You are raven bonkers.'
'I won't sink as low as you.'
'But to settle this dispute, I
Know the thing we ought to do.'

And so, back to back, they started,
Paced away, and then took flight,
Seeing which one could fly higher.
That would settle it alright.

Upward Ronald soared, majestic,
Knowing he had won the score.
He had seventeen primary pinions.
Vel had lost. Ron had one more.

One more wing quill really mattered.
It had made the crow a minion.
After all the two and eights,
It was a difference of a pinion.

© December 2020

TWO SMALL SPARROWS

In a small garden in the Netherlands
Stands a pavilion for exotic birds.
It's simply built of canopy and wire,
And parakeets fly joyfully inside.
Upon the floor, small quail importantly
Scrabble across the balding grass and dust.
And budgerigars perch high and make remarks,
As though nobody else but they can hear.
Outside, two sparrows go careering through the trees.
They have a nest within the cool beech hedge.
For just a moment, they swoop down to drink
In a crock bowl that nestles in the grass.
The parakeets are happy with their lot.
Safe in their palace, nothing troubles them.
Their food is brought, fresh gathered, every day.
But oh, they can't resist a little jibe.
'You may think you are free and we are caged.
But we are loved more preciously than you.
Nothing can harm us in our pleasure dome,
Whilst you have been abandoned and forgot.'
The sparrows smile and do not say a word,
Although they hear those words upon the breeze.
They dance across the garden to their nest,
Knowing that they are also loved and blessed.

© May 2011

CHAFF
(CHIFFCHAFF)

When Dickens gets together
With his friends for light repast,
They soon indulge in badinage,
Bright, witty, light and fast.
No malice is intended,
And indeed, it isn't there.
But only gentle teasing
And kind humour fills the air.

They call this verbal jostling,
Which brings many a fulsome laugh,
A funny little word, and that word
Flies like winnowed chaff.
In fact that is the name they give.
Though it might seem absurd,
They call their conversation
For a tiny olive bird.

Well not entirely olive,
But a little bit more brown,
He flits around the trees
And, while he bobbles up and down,
He sings a little ditty,
That is of no consequence,
But it sounds so fine and pretty,
And could never give offence.

And so Victorian gentlemen
And chiffchaffs share a theme.
Their words and song don't chafe.
Of that faux pas they would not dream.
They sip their tea, these learnéd men,
And talk of love and fate,
And all the while the chiffchaff
Warbles sweetly on the gate.

A BIT OF A DO
(ROOKS)

The rooks up at Thorley are prepping their nests.
They're cocking their beaks and they're puffing their chests.
They're so proud of their work on behalf of their eggs,
That they're posing like storks. But they don't have the legs.

The rooks up at Thorley are staking their claim,
So that all other residents know of their name.
There have been rooks at Thorley for ever so long.
If you think they're just blackbirds, you're ever so wrong.

The rooks up at Thorley are having a bash.
It's not very grand, 'cos there isn't much cash.
But what really counts is the getting together.
For that's what you do when you're birds of a feather.

The rooks up at Thorley are singing a ditty.
They open their beaks, but it's not very pretty.
For linnets or larks, they are never mistook.
But it's oh, such an honour, just being a rook.

© March 2006

THE PARROT OF THE SEA
(PUFFIN)

A wondrous bird, the puffin,
The parrot of the sea.
It skims the northern oceans,
With a cool efficiency.

They nestle down together
In giant colonies,
Which shield the cold wind's bitterness
Which whips from off the seas.

Around the Scottish Islands
They're protected by the law.
But in Faroes and in Iceland
Their hearts are eaten raw.

In fact, there was a time when,
With nothing else to eat,
They became a staple diet,
Not a delicacy meat.

But here within the British Isles,
We are a caring race,
And we would scorn to eat a bird
With such a jovial face.

So long may puffins flourish
On our far-flung British Isles,
Free from the threat of others,
Free to fill our hearts with smiles.

© January 2016

ESTONIAN STORKS

Of all the Estonian birdlife,
The storks are a curious lot.
The black ones are hard at their business,
But the white ones have clearly forgot.

They swagger about at their leisure.
They feed and they breed and they thrive,
Whilst pregnant Estonian ladies
Wonder when will their babies arrive?

Meanwhile, at the 'new baby' depot,
The nappies are fast running out.
It is time to send out a message.
What is the delay all about?

The storks are, at last, reprimanded
And each take a baby in beak
And now the Estonian birthrate
Is rising, at last, as we speak.

BEATING A PATHWAY TO PARADISE
(SWANS)

On a dark and dismal morning,
Christmastime close to the eye,
I espied three swans a-sailing,
In formation, through the sky,
Necks outstretched, like fingers, pointing
To a place they could not see,
Destined ever to gaze onwards
Past our world of misery.

Now I wonder if I saw you.
You were such a magic sight,
As you took your dreams before you,
Single-minded in your flight.
Yet, if I should listen quietly,
And life's fury cease to ring,
I might hear my heart in rhythm
With the beat of downy wing.

© 1994

ICARUS FEASTING
(WAXWINGS)

We walked the streets of Tromsø,
On that grey and chilly day.
But, in turning round a corner,
Something took our breath away.
We saw a ring of crimson,
Staining bright the foot-crushed snow,
From a tree of blood-bright berries,
Which had made the morning glow.
And there, seated in the branches,
Feasting as if life near ended,
Were a flock of brilliant waxwings,
Upon which the tree depended.
Their splash of ruby colour
Matched the bounty of the tree.
And their gold shone like the absent sun,
Or so it seemed to me.
The camera kept failing.
For the cold had drained it dry.
But I had to catch that miracle
Before I passed it by.
And at last the picture took;
That joyful gathering of birds.
But I knew that I could trap it
Much more tenderly with words.

© March 2013

ACORN EATER
(JAY)

The oak trees stand, as they always do,
Like the ents of the Tolkein tale.
Their verdant tresses are thinning out
To a yellow and amber veil.
But promise is clustered beneath the locks,
As the fruit coffers overflow.
And the gatherers of the Harvest come
To the happiest feast that they know.
A flash of ginger streaks through the boughs
To gather the acorn boon.
He pull the nuts from their natal cups
Through the warmth of the afternoon.
Some will be polished off there and then.
But some will go underground,
Until the snows of the winter come
And no other fare can be found.
The acorn eater will relocate
Nine oak seeds in every ten.
The rest will sprout in the open ground,
To become a woodland again.
The Spring will bring newness in every form.
As it marches through, day by day.
And, fed by the seeds from the great oak trees,
So flourish the young of the Jay.

© 10th October 2008

TERN OF THE TIDE
(LITTLE TERN)

A little tern was wandering
Along the briny strand.
A saunter on our stormy shores
Was not quite what he planned.
For this was not the time of year
When he should be around.
Australia and South Africa
Were where he should be found.

The little tern was getting on
In terms of birdy years.
His memory was not so good,
And he had many fears.
But God, who'd seen his sorry plight,
Put wind beneath his wings
And lifted him into the sky
To guide his wanderings.

The little tern was carried
On the strong, persistent breeze,
Until he saw South Africa
And landed there with ease.
The sun was warm and comforting,
And all along the sand
Were all his friends from yesteryear
A-nestling in the sand.

There was his mother with her brood,
Before they'd even hatched.
And gulls that circled overhead
Were speedily dispatched.
And love was landing everywhere
And everything was nice.
There would be no more wandering.
He'd come to Paradise.

© *March 2019*

BIRD

Bird. What an enigmatic word.
From out the mists of time they came,
The Archaeopteryx, the Dodo and the Auk.
In fantasy, the Phoenix braved the flames,
And they still talk about the Raven, and the Dove,
Symbolic of God's love.
Upon a Peacock throne once sat an emperor.
And pigeons brought back hope to those at home.
And children chanted rhymes of long ago.
Sing one for sorrow and sing two for joy.
A feathered head-dress for Red Indian boy.
Three feathers for a prince, swallows for Spring,
Heaven Hounds for Autumn, a nightingale to sing.
Whisper of battery hens and fighting cocks,
And partridge shoots, marauding fox.
A quill to write. An owl to hoot at night.
Owls may seem wise. But we are only fools.
Birds can fly free. But we just break the rules.
We try to be like them. We seek the skies;
To see the bird's-eye view, as the crow flies.
But, just as Icarus flew too near the Sun,
We fail the test before we have begun.
The ugly duckling that can never change.
We spoil our world. We kill the Albatross.
And what should be our gain, is all our loss.

© 1986

ON THE KNIFE'S EDGE
(BLUE TIT)

A lovely sunny day; the sky so blue.
Hardly a hint of cloud to mar the view.
Yet, swaying branch-tips beckon everywhere.
They suck the meagre warmth out of the air.

Amongst the bramble arches, stout and strong,
A blue tit sings a sweet and plaintive song.
'Please bring it back, bring back the warmth to me.'
'I need the Spring to start my family.'

So it begins, the carousel of life.
As cold and warmth perch on an upturned knife
And one small soul might turn the blade and sing
And all the world could topple into Spring.

© March 2010